Oil & Gas Industry: Getting Kenya Past the Resource Curse

Yuvenalis Ogendi

Oil & Gas Industry: Getting Kenya Past the Resource Curse

LAP LAMBERT Academic Publishing

Imprint

Any brand names and product names mentioned in this book are subject to trademark, brand or patent protection and are trademarks or registered trademarks of their respective holders. The use of brand names, product names, common names, trade names, product descriptions etc. even without a particular marking in this work is in no way to be construed to mean that such names may be regarded as unrestricted in respect of trademark and brand protection legislation and could thus be used by anyone.

Cover image: www.ingimage.com

Publisher:
LAP LAMBERT Academic Publishing
is a trademark of
International Book Market Service Ltd., member of OmniScriptum Publishing Group
17 Meldrum Street, Beau Bassin 71504, Mauritius

ISBN: 978-620-2-07797-2

Copyright © Yuvenalis Ogendi
Copyright © 2019 International Book Market Service Ltd., member of OmniScriptum Publishing Group

DEDICATION

For my family and friends, given and chosen.

Contents

ABBREVIATIONS AND ACRONYMS

BP   British Petroleum

EAC   East African Community

ECT   Energy Charter Treaty

EITI   Extractive Industries Transparency Initiative

ERC   Energy Regulatory Commission

GDP   Gross Domestic Product

IBA   Impact Benefit Agreement

NERC   National Energy Regulatory Commission

NNPC   Nigerian National Petroleum Corporation

NOCK   National Oil Corporation of Kenya

OIEP   Oil Exploration and Production Company

OMCs   Oil Marketing Companies

ABSTRACT

Kenya has joined the list of countries in the oil and gas sector after a successful prospecting with production slated to start in 2019. With the obvious expectations, it is imperative that such discovery is accompanied by an already established and effective legal framework to seamlessly regulate the upstream oil and gas sector.

With the recent discovery of oil and gas resources in Kenya, this paper contextualizes the resource curse from a legal perspective. A critical analysis of the legislative framework in relation to the oil and gas sector in the upstream stage is evaluated. The paper concludes that under the current legal arrangement and the proposed legislation in relation to the upstream oil and gas sector, the recent discovery of oil and gas resource in Kenya will offer no difference from similar African countries that have been victims of the resource curse. Drawing from a critical evaluation of the provisions in the Kenyan legislative framework and that from selected case studies, the analysis asserts that a legislative framework that takes into account the unique primordial features of a country is critical in steering a country past the resource curse.

Further to this, a succinct conclusion has been provided with recommendations on how the oil and gas sector can handle the impacts that come with oil and gas resources.

ACKNOWLEDGMENT

My heartfelt gratitude to Mrs. Caroline Kago, my dissertation supervisor for her endless and invaluable guidance, her non-obligated corrections and timely recommendations throughout the entire writing of this work

My divine appreciation for my family members, dad George, mom Martha, brother Edwin, sisters Winnie and Lucy.

Thanks to the University of Ghana for hosting me through the proposal stage of this work, the Global Development Network for faith in my vision and perseverance through my endless research.

Massive gratitude to Dzidza for the notable additions, Evans for the edits made and Simplice Asongu for the ready support

Credit: Akintunde Akinleye, Reuters (2012

1.0 Chapter one: Background Information

1.1 Introduction

The recent discovery of oil and gas in Kenya[1] has necessitated the engagement in a number of legal transformations[2]. However, many challenges still lie in the way of the country's bid for a successful development of its oil and gas industry. Unless the legal and institutional weaknesses are addressed at the earliest opportunity, the revenues derived from the exploration of the industry could turn into a curse: the resource curse. The country would be an additional statistic to the resource curse. Sachs and Warner[3] find in their definitive study that countries with significant natural resources tend to grow more slowly than resource-poor countries. This paper focuses on the potential negative impact of natural resources from the discovered oil and gas fields as a result of a weak and inadequate legal framework.

Governments play an exceptionally significant role in the resource sectors of arguably all developing countries and, at least in theory, have the legal tools to mitigate each of these hardships through the legislative arm. The Rentier theory of law[4] holds that mineral rents reduce the necessity of the government to levy domestic taxes, rendering leaders less accountable to citizens and more prone to rent-seeking, corruption and patronage politics. The legislative arm of

---

[1] Oil exploration is still ongoing in order to define the extent of the oil and gas reserves (Tullow Oil, 2013)

[2] The proposed Energy Bill is in its advanced fifth draft stage and is set to be the major piece of legislation handling the energy sector in Kenya alongside the provisions of the Constitution of Kenya, 2010.

[3] Sachs,J.,and A.Warner(1995) *Natural Resource Abundance and Economic Growth*." Development Discussion Paper pp. 151-162. No. 517a, Harvard Institute for International Development.

[4] The relationship between law and the states that derive considerable portions of their national revenues from the amounts collected from indigenous resources to foreign clients.

government that is concerned with law making is comprised of these leaders same leaders who have been tasked with managing the energy industry.

Kenya has the potential of becoming a hydrocarbon producer and an oil exporter in the coming years[5]. The results are twofold: on the one hand, if the oil and gas industry is efficiently managed, this offers the country a unique opportunity to stimulate its economic industry.[6] However, on the other hand, mismanagement of the resources will add the East African country to the list of African states that have fallen prey to the resource curse.[7]

There has been an unprecedented interest in the Kenyan upstream oil and gas sector. This follows the discoveries of oil in the neighboring Uganda and the offshores of East Africa[8]. The principal players are Tullow Oil in partnership with Africa Oil and Centric Energy. The four core concentrations of this dissertation will be the Lamu Basin, the Anza Basin, the Mandera Basin and the Tertiary Rift Basin[9]. These basins mark the focal primary Production Sharing Contracts

---

[5] On 26th March 2012, Tullow Oil announced successful discovery of oil deposits at Ngamia-1 well located In Turkana County. There has been a series of discovery of oil in the area, the latest being the Agete-1 Wildcat well, the fifth in the chain of oil discovery in the area. Accessed from
http://www.tullowoil.com/index.asp?pageid=137&year=Latest&month=&filtertags=84&selected=
[Accessed: 26 April, 2015].
[6] According to the School of Diplomacy and International Relations at Seton Hall University, the potential to simulate the economy based on the oil and gas resources is unlimited. A study by the program contends that over the last decade, African Oil producing counties benefited from a spectacular jump in oil prices, which rose from $22 per barrel in 2003 to $147 per barrel in 2008 and remained high, for the most part, until recently. The spoils were enormous: from 2002 to 2012, Angola's GDP jumped from $11 billion to $114 billion and Nigeria's went from $59 billion to $243 billion.
[7] From a legal perspective, the resource curse mirrors the situation where the countries and regions that have an abundance of natural resources with specific reference to non-renewable resources including oil and gas tend to display lesser economic growth rates and worse development outcomes as compared to countries with fewer natural resources, primarily as a result of the decline in the competitiveness of other sectors in the same economy (Tullow Oil, 2013)
[8] http://www.geoexpro.com/articles/2014/09/oil-and-gas-exploration-in-east-africa-a-brief-history
[9] Please see figure 1 at 1.1.2.

that have been signed with the Kenyan government[10]. This is to be legally analyzed against the success that the concept of Devolution[11] seeks to bring to the country.

The key institutions in Kenya that are involved in the regulation of the upstream oil and gas sector are currently the Ministry of Energy and the National Oil Corporation of Kenya (NOCK).[12]With the upsurge in interest and no separate industry regulator, this paper seeks to examine whether the legal framework in place which is principally made up of the Constitution of Kenya 2010, [13]the Petroleum (Exploration and Production) Act,[14] chapter 308 of the Laws of Kenya (the Petroleum Act),[15] regulations made under the Petroleum Act and the Ninth Schedule to the Income Tax Act, chapter 470 of the Laws of Kenya have the capacity to steer the country away from the resource curse and into economic prosperity. Further, the proposed Energy Bill[16] provisions will be critically examined This is particularly so with the current powers of the Minister for Energy as provided for under the Petroleum Act and the Constitutional provisions in relation to the National Land Commission having overlapping undertones.

---

[10] *http://www.ogj.com/oil-exploration-and-development/discoveries.html.* [Accessed: 7 April, 2015].

[11] Transparency International Kenya (2013) *Towards Hazy Horizons. An opinion poll on the implementation of Devolution and governance reforms in Kenya,* (Nairobi: Transparency International Kenya.)
http:/www.tikenya.org/index.php/press-releases/222-towards-hazy-horizons-an-opinion-poll-on-implementation-of-Devolution-and-governance-reforms-in-kenya (accessed 17 October 2014)

[12] NOCK is wholly owned by the government of Kenya and acts as an instrument of government policy in matters that relate to oil and gas. The company also gives advice to Kenyan energy policymakers. It was established primarily to facilitate and participate in the exploration of petroleum products in the country.

[13] This provides for the establishment of the National Land Commission and for the ratification of grants of rights or concessions regarding the exploitation of natural resources by parliament.

[14] The Petroleum Act provides that all minerals and mineral oils shall vest in the national government in trust for the people of Kenya. However, under the Constitution, the administration of the minerals and mineral oils shall be vested in the National Land Commission.

[15] Petroleum (Exploration and Production) Act, Chapter 308. (Revised Edition 2012). Nairobi: National Council of Law Reporting with the Authority of the Attorney General.

[16] Available at http://www.kengen.co.ke/documents/National%20Energy%20Policy%20-%20Final%20Draft%20-%2027%20Feb%202014.pdf

3

1.1.1 Kenya's Four Hydrocarbon Basins

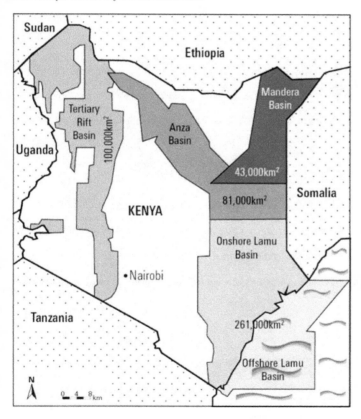

Source: Heya (2012)

1.2 Statement of the problem

Weak legal frameworks have always been credited with the adverse impacts that characterize states battling the resource curse[17]. The principal goal of this research is to analyze whether the legal framework in place can prevent a resource curse in Kenya. This is undertaken given that the legal framework in place and the contemplated legislation[18] mirror the provisions of the states that form case studies for this research and which have been cited as having encountered the resource curse.

This analysis undertakes to evaluate whether the legislation provides for transparency in its dealings with the mining, oil and gas companies, provides for tougher disclosure and anti-corruption legislation and whether the economic policies as interpreted within the existent legal contexts promote for the diversification of the economies as well as discourage the dependence on the resource revenues as the major factors that have been presented as measures to avoid the resource curse[19].

---

[17] Jorge E. Viñuales (*2011*) *The Resource Curse: A Legal Perspective. Global Governance*: A Review of Multilateralism and International Organizations: April-June 2011, Vol. 17, No. 2, pp. 197-212.
[18] Proposed Energy Bill, 2014
[19] Legal policy measures as provided for by the Extractive Industries Transparency Initiative

1.3 Theoretic Framework

This research work principally assumes a socio-legal approach as a derivative of the pure theory of law[20]. The paper contends that the supposed Grundnorm for the effectiveness of the oil and gas sector particularly in Africa is based on an efficient legal framework and the bodies tasked with the implementation. The failure of these steps is what leads to the resource curse.

The selected countries for case studies are directly involved in the resource curse owing to inadequate legal frameworks. In 2010, Equatorial Guinea had a per capita income of $35 000 which was the continents highest. However, up to 75% of the population lived on less than $700 a year. In South Sudan where the oil revenues account for more than 18% of the GDP and Nigeria where the funds account for up to 30% of the GDP, civil strife and conflict has been rife particularly in the oil-producing regions.[21]

Since the exploration is in its preliminary phase, this work will be a critical analysis of the legislation that has been established or is contemplated being established,[22] the role of devolution in ensuring that the production and exploration is successful and a comparison with the selected case studies. The paper seeks to advance the cause that Kenya adopts the success story that has been experienced in Botswana in relation to natural resource exploration. The theoretical spirit is definitely present. What is of grave concern, however, is the implementation approach that will be adopted by key players: the legal framework and institutional mechanisms.

---

[20] The 'Pure Theory of Law' by Kelsen is a theory of Positive Law and not of a specific legal order. See Pure Theory of Law, retrieved from http://www.science.uva.nl/~seop/entries/lawphil-theory/ (accessed on 20 January, 2015) Notably, two points are that: the Grundnorm is not the same thing as the constitution, and that the historically first constitution is often indeed just – the root of legitimacy in the current constitutional order

[21] Freedom House has listed only five of the twenty top oil producing countries as "free". In a majority of the countries, it was found that the important checks that were previously present in relation to monitoring abuse of power by the government such as civil societies and democratic cultures to be in short supply.

[22] Energy Bill 2014

This research is heavily influenced by the legal gap in understanding and addressing the occurrence that the natural resources have traditionally been associated with particularly on the African continent. The only case exception seems to be Botswana as shall be illustrated in the case studies. The issue of corruption and how it fuels the resource curse will also be analyzed. The Republic of Congo has the highest total resource rents as percentage of GDP in Africa (64%) and one of the lowest index scores of corruption. Equatorial Guinea, with a government widely seen as autocratic, has the worst control of corruption score among African countries. It also has very high resource rents as a share of GDP, at 47%.[23]

1.4 Hypothesis

This study tests the hypothesis that unless Kenya, particularly on legal policy formulation, adopts a proper and tailored legal framework as opposed to duplicating provisions from other oil states in its approach to its nascent oil and gas sector, then the natural resource discovery will lead to economy stagnation and by extension the resource curse as opposed to spurring economic growth and prosperity. The following will be formulated for the research:

H0: That Kenya's upstream oil and gas sector success or failure is pegged on the legal framework

H1: That Kenya's upstream oil and gas sector success or failure is not pegged on the legal framework

---

[23] Lawson-Remer, Terra. "The Centre on Foreign Relations: African perspective." 3 August 2012. Council on Foreign Relations. 16 September 2014 <http://www.centreonforeignrelations.com>.

1.5 Objective of the study

The foundation of this research work will be evaluating the legal history of oil exploration in Kenya, the legal framework in place, the contemplated legislation[24], the nexus between legislative influence on oil and oil curse in Africa[25] with case studies of Equatorial Guinea,[26] South Sudan, Nigeria and Botswana, the role of civil society and citizenry and whether the framework currently in place; with specific regard to the legal framework, have the capacity to prevent the traditional Oil curse in Africa from replicating itself.

1.6 Significance of the study

This research is carried out to appraise the effect of the upstream oil and gas legislative framework. The need of the study is to analyze the adverse effect of an inadequate legal framework in harnessing the discovered oil fields in spurring the economic growth of the country.

The research is expected to be of benefit to the stakeholders in the oil and gas sector in Kenya, particularly in recommendations for the draft Energy Bill and the draft National Energy Policy.

---

[24] Analysis of the provisions of the draft Energy Bill 2014

[25] 'Lifting the Natural Resource Curse' www.globalpolicy.org (Retrieved 2014-10-19)

[26] Boasting of one billion barrels of oil reserves, Equatorial Guinea has been recorded to export as much as 400 000 barrels of oil every day since the year 1995. In terms of GDP per capita, these reserves make the country wealthier than France, the United Kingdom and Japan. However, according to the United Nations Statistics Division, despite such wealth, three out of every four Equatorial Guineans live on less than $2 a day. The infant mortality rates have remained to be high since the first discovery of oil in the region.

1.7 Research Questions

1. Does the legal framework in place have the capacity to handle the upsurge of interest in the industry with a focus on conflict resolution and accountability[27]?

2. Is the National Oil and Gas Policy for Kenya merely a wish list? Is it a statement of intent rather than a practical step to exploit the harness the oil and gas resources for the people of Kenya?

3. How can the legislative framework in the oil and gas sector be aligned to avoid for conflict in oil and gas resources and duplication of roles?

4. How effectively will the critical concerns and challenges that are as a result of the exploration activity in the oil and gas sector in Kenya be addressed?

1.8. Resource curse: Legal perspective

This research adopts a legal perspective to the resource curse by providing a matrix of the legal framework of an oil and gas producing country, or its absence in explaining the resource curse.

1.9. Literature Review

In *Oil, development and the politics of the bottom billion*,[28] the oil and gas discovery in Kenya has been christened to offer the possibility of two scenarios: economic growth if managed well or the resource curse in the event of mismanagement. There is extensive literature that has sought to define the context of the resource curse. This position is contended by Branch in *Kenya:*

---

[27] The exploitation of any natural resource is subject to ratification by parliament. This must be done by the 28th, August 2014 to meet the five year period spelt out. It is uncertain what such ratification will have on the future grant of rights that have been provided for under the Petroleum Act. It is to be noted that the ratifications will only affect future transactions. What then becomes of the current transactions given the length of the exploration contacts?

[28] Watts M. (2009) '*Oil, development, and the politics of the bottom billion*', Macalester International, 24, Article 11, pp. 79-130

Between Hope and Despair.[29] However, while the authors have addressed the resource curse in Africa, they have failed to evaluate the role that has been played by the weak legal frameworks of the failed countries and their accompanying implementing bodies. The literature review has further failed by offering a generalized comparison of the legal framework of the countries without providing an explanation of the country's current situation.

Ross, in *Does Oil Hinder Democracy*[30] elucidates on the close relationship that exists between the harnessing of oil and gas resources within the legal framework of a country. With a focus on African countries, the book offers a validation on the need for the alignment of all laws governing the management of oil and gas resources. The analysis however, fails on two fundamental premises. First, Ross argues that the upstream oil and gas sector is fundamentally a confine of the government. This is not the case since the contracts are signed by oil companies on behalf of the government. In the Kenyan case, Tullow Oil and Partners is the contracted company. Secondly, the discourse assumes an already established legal framework for the upstream oil and gas sector. The general African, and particular Kenyan situation position indicates that the legal policies are in the process of being drafted[31].

The major definition has seemingly mirrored the approach of state failure, an increase in the levels of civil disorder and poor economic performances being recorded as was posited in Humphrey's Journal of *Natural Resources, Conflict and Conflict Resolution.*[32] The preparedness

[29] Branch, D. (2011) *Kenya: Between Hope and Despair, 1963-2011* (New Haven and London: Yale University Press)
[30] Ross, Michael, L. (2001a). *Does Oil Hinder Democracy*? World Politics 53: 325-61.
[31] The draft Energy Bill, 2014 and the draft National Energy Policy
[32] Humphreys, M. (2005) 'Natural Resources, Conflict and Conflict Resolution', *Journal of Conflict Resolution*, 49 (4), pp. 508–537, DOI: 10.1177/0022002705277545 DOI : 10.1177/0022002705277545

of the institutional framework in place borders primarily on the Devolution[33] process, where the local governments will be empowered to address the local needs. The general consensus finds that where the oil production takes place in countries characterized by weak legal institutions and where such reserves are located populated by marginalized groups with deep grievances to the government, then the chances of violent conflicts are higher, as explained by Karl in *The Paradox of Plenty: Oil Booms and Petro States*[34]. The shortcoming, however, stems from the narrow typological categorization of the parameters that are used in the measurement of the resource curse.

In 2011, the top eight oil producers on the continent were Nigeria, Algeria, Egypt, Libya, Sudan, Angola, the Republic of Congo and Equatorial Guinea. According to the World Bank, the last decade has posted a negative score on the World Bank's control of corruption index. Every one of the said countries has been hit by either a violent conflict or a repressive regime. The Summary Report: *Avoiding the Resource Curse and advancing the Human Rights within the Oil and Gas sector in Kenya*[35] presented at the Intercontinental Hotel on 6th November, 2012 highlights that it is possible to avoid the resource curse. This is further supported by a number of transcript of papers presented at an international conference in New Delhi in June 2008 hosted jointly by the Institute for Defence Studies and Analyses and International Peace Research Institute, Oslo, focusing on Energy contend that the African setup with legal frameworks that govern land ownership in countries that harness natural resources allow for the government to

---

[33] *Daily Nation* (2013)*President Uhuru's tough agenda for Kenya,*, 16 April,http://www.nation.co.ke/News/President-Uhuru-tough-agenda-for-Kenya/-/1056/1750098/-/vvjblc/-/index.html#comment-865186250 (accessed 18 October 2014).

[34] The coming oil boom in Africa is paradoxically a frightening prospect for the continent's poor and marginalized Karl T. L. (1997) *The Paradox of Plenty. Oil Booms and Petro States*.(Berkeley-Los Angeles-London: University of California Press).

[35] Nyoike, P. M. (2012) *Outlook of Oil and Gas Exploration Status in Kenya*, East Africa Upstream Summit, Nairobi, 25-26 October.

quickly remove the people living in the way of the extractive activities.[36] This is another point that might lead to conflict if not adequately addressed by the legal provisions.

Petroleum Exploration Overview in Kenya[37] further serves to highlight the crucial role that a strong and effective legal framework as supplemented by equally reliable institutions play in steering a country away from the resource curse. It has however failed to acknowledge the integrity that is to be associated with the drafting process.

Stevens, in *Resource Impact: Curse or Blessing?*[38] Emphasizes on the need for a clear distinction between the expectations of the people and particularly those living in the areas where the resource discovery has been made. This assertion has been adopted in this paper with an additional conclusion on the need for codifying such provisions.

1.10. Research Methodology

The principal source for this research work will be the vast literature review that is available on the topic under study. This will form the bulk of the methodology. The writer will also have the access to relevant conferences and workshops organized to discuss matters that relate to the oil and gas sector in Kenya. Further to this, interviews with key players and stakeholders in the area will offer a practical perspective to the study. In addition to the above, direct observation especially through media commentary will supplement the primary methodologies.

---

[36] Syagga, P. (2006) 'Land Ownership and Use in Kenya: Policy Prescriptions from an Inequality Perspective', *Readings in Inequality in Kenya*, Sectoral Dynamics and Perspectives, Volume 1, pp. 291-330.
[37] Heya, M. (May 10, 2012) *Petroleum Exploration Overview in Kenya*, Presentation at the 19th Engineers International Conference. Ministry of Energy, Kenya,http://www.powershow.com/view/3b0097-NzgxM/19TH_ENGINEERS_INTERNATIONAL_CONFERENCE_powerpoint_ppt_presentation(accessed 12 October 2014).
[38] Stevens, Paul. (2003*). Resource Impact: Curse or Blessing*? A Literature Survey. Journal of Energy Literature 9 (1): 3-42.

1.11. Chapter outline

This research is made up of five chapters.

1.11.1. CHAPTER ONE

This chapter provides a background and introduction to the research topic. The parameters that will be adopted for the purposes of the paper are set out given that the paper focuses on the upstream oil and gas sector.

1.11.2. CHAPTER TWO: The Constitutional and Legislative Essentials of   Exclusive ownership and regulation of Oil and Gas Resources of Kenya

This chapter is principally the backbone of this research paper. The existing institutions, current legal framework, the proposed legislation and primarily the Energy Bill will be analyzed.

This discourse will highlight the apparent overlap of roles and potential conflict of proprietary rights over oil and gas resources in Kenya, pegged on the provisions of the existing legislation and clear on the ambiguous provisions of the Energy Bill.

1.11.3. CHAPTER THREE: Comparative Legal Case study analysis

This chapter focuses on the identified countries as case studies. This will involve an analysis of their institutions and legal provisions governing the oil and gas industry.

1.11.4. CHAPTER FOUR: Impact Benefit Agreements.

This chapter will explore the legitimacy of the expectations of the local populations, the Kenyans and will seek to input human right issues that might arise with such expectations. Further, the chapter analyzes the Product Sharing Contracts clauses signed by prospecting companies and the local community.

1.11.5. CHAPTER FIVE: Conclusion and Recommendations

This chapter provides a conclusion that has been adopted by the paper drawing from the legal analysis and offers legal recommendations that have been identified as solutions to the gaps in the upstream oil and gas sector in order to avoid the resource curse.

2.0. Chapter Two

2.1. GOVERNANCE: THE CONSTITUTIONAL AND LEGISLATIVE ESSENTIALS OF EXCLUSIVE OWNERSHIP AND REGULATION OF OIL AND GAS RESOURCES IN KENYA.

2.1.1 The apparent overlap in roles within the oil and gas sector

There is a consensus on the intrinsic and positive correlation between the legal framework quality and the development outcome of the resource extraction. A validation or refute of the resource curse hypothesis is fundamentally based on the assumption of the fact that the resource abundance is correlated with measures of development that stem from the legal framework of any state that has natural resources[39].

A keen evaluation of the proposed legislation, mainly the Energy Bill 2014, indicates that there is an apparent overlap of roles that have the potential of leading to conflicts primarily from the proprietary rights over the oil and gas resources in the country. It is worth noting that the only laws that deal with the ownership of oil and gas resources in Kenya are the 2010 Constitution and the Petroleum Act Cap 308 Laws of Kenya.

---

[39] Frynas, Jedrezej, E. 2004. *The Oil Boom in Equatorial Guinea*. African Affairs 103 (413): 527-546.

14

The matrix of apparent overlap specifically affects the roles and the proprietary mandate that exist between parliament, the national government, the county government and the National Land Commission which has been listed as an independent body. Under this regard, each of the organs has been assigned roles by the legislative framework and thus raises the concern of supremacy despite the apparent weight that has been afforded to the provisions of the Constitution of Kenya, Article 2(1)[40]

2.1.2 Upstream oil and gas sector

This research focuses on the upstream oil and gas sector in Kenya. The division is commonly referred to as the exploration and production sector. This refers to the search, recovery and production of crude oil and natural gas. The major steps that are involved within this sector include the search for underground or underwater oil and gas fields, the drilling of exploratory wells and, if the wells are deemed economically viable and recoverable, the operation of wells that bring crude oil and natural gas to the well's surface[41].

It is worth mentioning that the subsequent midstream sector involves the gathering of the systems for the storage of the oil and gas resources while the downstream sector refers to the process of refining the crude oil and sale as well as distribution of the by-products of the crude oil.

---

[40] This constitution is the supreme law of the Republic and binds all persons and all state organs at both levels of government
[41] http://www.psgdover.com/en/oil-and-gas/oil-gas-market-overview/oil-gas-upstream accessed 14 April 2015

2.1.3 Upstream oil and gas sector policy foundations

It is worth noting that the policy foundations for the extraction of oil are provided for in the Draft National Energy Policy[42]. This policy is yet to be adopted. With a particular focus on the upstream oil and gas sector, the Policy seeks to harness energy as a means of hastening the economic empowerment of the National and County governments.

2.2. The relevant laws on Oil Extraction in Kenya

The Constitution of Kenya, 2010 as the supreme law of the country makes provisions for oil extraction in the country. The other principal laws applicable include:

2.2.1. The Petroleum (Exploration and Production) Act, Chapter 308 of the Laws of Kenya

This Act was enacted to provide for regulation on the negotiations and conclusions reached by the government in agreements relating to the exploration for, development, production and transportation of petroleum.

2.2.2. The Petroleum Development Fund Act, Chapter 426C of the Laws of Kenya

This Act was enacted in 1991 with the primary goal of establishing a Petroleum Development Fund as well as the imposition of a Petroleum Development Levy.

2.2.3 The Draft National Energy Policy makes a number of provisions on the laws applicable in the oil sector. They include:

a) The Standards Act, Chapter 496 of the Laws of Kenya

---

[42] The Draft National Energy Policy available at:
http://www.kengen.co.ke/documents/National%20Energy%20Policy%20-%20Third%20Draft%20-%20May%2011%202012.pdf. [Accessed: 8 April, 2015]

This Act makes provision for the weights and measuring standards to be applied in matters involving oil and gas products for the purposes of resource allocation. Further, the minimum quality specifications have been articulated.

b) The Public Procurement and Disposal Act No. 3 of 2005

The preambular provision articulates for the definition of goods publicly procured to include oil and gas products.

c) The Anti-Corruption and Economic Crimes Act No.3 of 2003

d) The Public Officer Ethics Act No. 4 of 2003

e) The Land Act of 2012

f) The Environmental Management and Co-ordination Act of 1999

g) The Local Government Act, Chapter 265 of the laws of Kenya

h) The Land Registration Act, 2012

i) The Ethics and Anti-Corruption Commission Act No.22 of 2011

j) The Weights and Measures Act, Chapter 513 of the Laws of Kenya

2.3 The Constitution of Kenya, 2010

The Constitution of Kenya has a unique structure of ownership of oil and gas resources as compared to other jurisdictions. This uniqueness stems from the fact that it does not provide for an outright ownership scope of natural resources to any particular organ. This ambiguity is derived from the classification of natural resources as being part of 'public land' as defined under Article 62[43]. Therefore, oil and gas resources vest in and are held by the national government on a trust basis for the people of Kenya. They shall be managed by the National

---

[43]Public land is (f) all minerals and mineral oils as defined by the law

Land Commission. Article 237 of the Ugandan Constitution[44] and Article 89(5) of the Constitution of Ethiopia do not make a distinction between land and minerals as is the case in the Constitution of Kenya, 2010.

The constitution of Kenya, 2010 forms the basis for the government to exercise control over the natural resources under its jurisdictional control. Also, it is the constitution that preserves the rights of individuals as concerns the exploitation process. The state's involvement in oil and gas resource appropriation is made possible in three distinct ways: institutional measures[45], legislation and parliamentary oversight.

This paper's primary concern is centered on Article 71[46] which mandates the inclusion of parliamentary ratification of any reached agreements. The division of roles between the national and county government are marked out under the Fourth Schedule. Notably, the county government has been tasked with the vague[47] mandate of implementing the particular policies that have been advanced by the government.

The response of the Kenyan government in matters that have contentious elements has been predominantly to let matters paly out naturally for the sake of being politically correct. The aspect of parliamentary ratification might further have a detrimental effect given the partisan voting that has been a distinguishing factor of the National Assembly. As a concern, while a

---

[44] Constitution of Uganda

[45] The National Land Commission established under Article 67 is the expressly named institution. This has already been set up through the National Land Commission Act, No 5 of 2012

[46] (1) A transaction is subject to ratification by Parliament if It (a) involves the grant of a right or concession by or on behalf of any person, including the national government, to another person for the exploitation of any natural resource of Kenya

[47] The vagueness is in the sense that such enforcement is pegged on legislation that has not been effected yet and which does not have a timeline to its legislation.

legitimate company might win the prospecting, a green light is at the mercy of the current political situation which has a high influence on the parliamentary ratification process.

2.4 The Petroleum (Exploration and Production) Act[48]

The Petroleum Act is the most salient upstream oil and gas statute in the country. The Act was enacted with the primary reason of regulating the negotiation as well as conclusions of the agreements that have been reached by the government[49]. Section 3 of the Act provides the legal basis for the government's appropriation rights. This is provided as:

'All petroleum existing in its natural condition in strata lying within Kenya and the continental shelf is vested in the Government, subject to any rights in respect thereof which, by or under any other written law, have been or are granted or recognized as being vested, in any other person'

The analysis for this paper is the extraction of oil and gas which happens to be in the upstream sector. The stipulation under the Act is that any activities involving petroleum operations can only take place after the approval of the Minister in such a manner as has been prescribed by the Act[50]. The present cabinet allocation in Kenya places this mandate on the Cabinet Secretary for Energy and Petroleum.

Despite the fact that Article 62(3) of the Constitution of Kenya addresses the adjusted vested rights, it still remains to be seen whether the central government's role is unaffected even

---

[48] An Act enacted in 1984 that is bei9ng reviewed in the National Energy Policy
[49] The Petroleum Act under section 1 elaborates on the operations and they include exploration for development, extraction, production, separation and treatment, storage, transportation and sale or disposal of petroleum up to the point of export, or the agreed delivery point in Kenya or the point of entry into a refinery
[50] Section 4(1)

after the introduction of the administrative role of the National Land Commission. Further to this, the issue of trust ownership and the role of parliament in approving contractual appropriation of natural resources as posited under Article 71.

The right of appropriation is carried out by the government in three ways. The first is through management by its own National Oil Corporation while the second is through non state operators in the form of contractors. In Kenya, the National Oil Corporation is the National Oil Corporation of Kenya, a state corporation incorporated in April 1981 and which has been tasked exclusively with handling all petroleum matters. The Government of Kenya has a 100% ownership stake in the corporation. The third way is "in such manner as may be necessary or appropriate"[51]. It is worth noting that in the negotiation for the agreements, the best interests of the government are given first regard. Further to this, the Cabinet secretary has been conferred with the supervisory powers in matters carried out under the petroleum agreements reached.

Within this Act, the Minister remains an integral figure in the Oil exploration and production activities. Notably, as opposed to other statutes, this Act does not specify the meaning of Minister for its purposes. This thereby creates an interpretation gap, given that any of the ministers from the Ministry of Energy and Petroleum, Ministry of Environment, Water and Natural Resources and Ministry of Mining can lay claim on the basis of the Constitution.

2.5 The Energy Bill, 2014

The Energy Bill reviews the Energy Act of 2006. The proposed Energy Bill handles the issues of property rights in petroleum, petroleum resources management and sharing of petroleum

---

[51] Petroleum Act, section 4(3)

resources in Part five (V). Notably, section 133[52] mirrors the constitution in the sense that all the petroleum resources have been held by the national government on behalf of the people of Kenya. If implemented, this will be the principal piece of legislation governing upstream exploration as read alongside relevant provisions of the Constitution of Kenya by virtue of section 134 which provides that:

> 'All petroleum resources shall be managed in accordance with the provisions of the Constitution and this Act'.

Interestingly, the provisions on the sharing of petroleum resources do not acknowledge any provisions concerning Product Sharing Contracts that have been signed by the government and exploration companies. The sharing has been allocated to three major recipients: the national government, the county government and the local community. The county government's share has been tagged at 20% of the government's share of the profit on oil. Further, of the 20% share, the county government has been obligated to allocate 25% of its share to the local community. While this provision seeks to provide a clear cut sharing process, it still remains fatal on two fundamental tiers: on the one hand, the provision has completely left out provisions relating to any allocations derived from the Product Sharing Contracts signed by the government to facilitate the process of exploration. Secondly, the provision does not accommodate for the legitimacy of the expectation of the local community in which the resources have been extracted.

Kenya being a country that has been demarcated arguably along ethnic grouping classification, the allocation of the profit share to all counties at the same share provides a legal hotspot. This is particularly so given that it is a requirement for any contractor involved in

---

[52] All petroleum existing in its natural condition in strata lying within Kenya and the continental shelf is vested in the national Government in trust for the people of Kenya, subject to any rights in respect thereof which, by or under any other written law, have been or are granted or recognized as being vested, in any other person.

petroleum explorations to ensure that the locals participate in every aspect of the operations. Under the Petroleum Act, there is an implied obligation that there will be a preference to Kenyan nationals in the petroleum operations.

In addition to the above, section 137(5)[53] on petroleum operations waters down the legal intensity by introducing a political dimension to the issue. This broad mandate on the government without any regulatory framework seems to imply a political supremacy to petroleum exploration, a matter that has been credited with the occurrence of the resource curse in most jurisdictions.

This paper finds it tragic, particularly with the wide discretionary powers that the cabinet secretary has been afforded. Notably, the Cabinet Secretary by virtue of section 5(3)(d) may make decisions that they consider to be desirable[54]. Given that there is no check and balance mechanism on the actions of the Cabinet Secretary, this makes the provision susceptible to abuse. Also liable to abuse is the fact that the power of signing or revoking the agreements reached can be done in either of two ways: by the secretary individually or a person that has been authorized in writing by the Cabinet Secretary[55].

The Kenyan Parliament has also been tasked with an integral responsibility in the issuance of permits for the exploration of natural resources within the country. This is in the

---

[53] Notwithstanding the provisions of this section, the Government may grant to any person, other than the contractor, a permit for the prospecting and mining of minerals or other natural resources other than petroleum or the conduct of operations other than petroleum operations within an area which is the subject of a petroleum agreement, provided that the prospecting, mining and the other operations shall not interfere with Petroleum operations.

[54] The Cabinet Secretary may take any action, decision, or give any permission or consent or exercise any other control as may be necessary or desirable for the purposes of the Act or the regulations made thereunder.

[55] Section 5(4)

22

sense that any transaction involving the grant or concession needs the ratification of parliament[56] , as discussed in the earlier part of this paper.

This chapter concludes that while there has been a legitimate attempt at drafting and enacting laws to regulate the upstream oil and gas sector, such drafting has not been aligned with the provisions as set out in the Constitution of Kenya. Further, such laws are fragmented and as such create a lacuna in terms of their applicability and the scope of applicability.

---

[56] Ibid, Article 71(1)

3.0. CHAPTER THREE

3.1 COMPARATIVE LEGAL CASE STUDY ANALYSIS

Kenya has joined the list of states that will soon be producing oil and gas in Africa. With the Third Summit on the exploration of oil and gas in East Africa slated for the third week of October 2015 in Nairobi, this chapter compares the Kenyan situation with selected countries based on their legal framework.

The selected countries have been used as case studies principally because they all have extractive sectors with legal frameworks providing for the same. While emphasis has been made on the African countries, Norway has been specially analyzed due to its standout upstream legislation. Further to this, the examination has been premised on the already established legal framework.

With the adoption and progressive implementation of the devolved system of government under the Constitution, the energy sector has not been adequately provided for. The tragedy of this is that it provides a breeding point for the County Governments to make laws that have extreme disparities over the same subject matters with the Central government, over the same matters.

According to data from the Oil and Gas Journal[57] the year 2013 on daily oil production per barrel, the following African countries lead the pack:

Country	No. of barrels annually
Nigeria	2.2 million
Algeria	2.1 million
Angola	1.9 million
Libya	1.7 million
Egypt	680,000
Southern Sudan	487,000
Equatorial Guinea	346,000

Source: Oil and Gas Journal, 2014

Collier and Anke[58] contend that oil rich nations are faced with conflict gaps in the form of civil wars and silent genocides primarily because the discoveries and exploration was not accompanied by legal updates to accompany such sectors. Instead, a majority of the states duplicate legal provisions from other states which do not augment well with the circumstances of that country. Further, the exploration of oil and gas is characterized by ecological disintegration as a result of the hazardous wastes. Interestingly, most legal provisions on oil and gas exploration do not make room for environmental considerations, and in the event that this is considered, it is usually a peripheral consideration which is not substantive to the legal draft.

---

[57] Oil and Gas Journal, Vol 98, Issue 11.
[58] Collier, Paul and Anke Hoeffler (2000). *Greed and Grievance in Civil War*. Policy Research Working Paper 2355. Washington DC: World Bank

Botswana which is rich in diamonds has been cited as one of the only African countries to avoid the resource curse. It is worth noting that while being a mineral, this case study has been used since it is an extractive natural resource, a similarity with the upstream oil and gas sector. In the year 2013, it was the wealthiest per capita country in Africa.

The Mining law in Botswana is governed by the Mines and Minerals Act, Cap 66:01 of the Laws of Botswana. With regard to the environmental impacts of all mining issues, the country has enacted the Environmental Assessment Act, Cap 65:07 of the Laws of Botswana. This has further been sub divided from any prospecting and the mining activities which lead to the discoveries of the minerals being prospected. Interestingly, matters to deal with Petroleum Exploration are covered separately under the Petroleum (Exploration and Production) Act, Cap 67:01 of the Laws of Botswana. Under the energy system in Botswana, two types of licences are recognized and these include one that covers exploration and one the covers development licences.

The above analysis of the legal framework governing oil and gas exploration in Botswana point to the fact that every aspect has been divided, and this is in the following main areas:

1. Laws governing the environmental impact of exploration
2. Laws governing the prospecting of mineral and petroleum products
3. Petroleum Exploration in the upstream sector

Within the Kenyan system, the Petroleum Act is the current major piece of legislation involved in all aspects of mining as read with the Constitution provisions and the Mining Bill which is currently reviewing the Mining Act. However, the review is at a stalemate owing to contentions over aspects on royalties. The proposed Energy Bill, pending approval, will take over the role of being the major piece of legislation. It is worth noting that all the major aspects are covered under one draft in either of these documents.

While it might be naïve to argue that the success story that has been experienced by Botswana in terms of its energy industry is a direct result of specific and distinct categorization of the roles and responsibilities of different agencies, it has a highly influential legal basis. With regard to the Kenyan case, the work practices on natural gas have been exclusively left to the discretion of the contractor by virtue of the provision under section 144[59]. Both jurisdictions have the similarity in the sense that laws affecting land tenure and the creation of security interests have both been adequately covered.

Once a prospecting licence has been granted to a company, the licence is subjected to the submission of a bankable feasibility study to the minister. While this provision is absent in the current Kenyan system, the proposed Energy Bill offers a security for compliance by virtue of section 151[60].Once this has been approved, the licence is issued for a period of three years with a renewal provision of up to a further two terms.

Sierra Leone which is similarly rich in diamonds seems to be resource cursed. While this has primarily been credited to the almost non-existent legal system which allowed for armed gangs[61] to exploit the country's rich diamond fields, the issue has persistently dogged the country

---

[59] A contractor shall carry out petroleum operations in the block in a proper and safe manner and in accordance with good oil field practices and take all reasonable steps necessary to secure the safety, health and welfare of persons engaged in those operations in or about the block and the contractor shall, in particular, but without prejudice to the generality of the foregoing.

[60] A petroleum agreement shall require a contractor to provide the Cabinet Secretary, prior to signing the petroleum agreement, performance bond issued in the form of an irrevocable bank guarantee by a reputable bank acceptable to the Cabinet Secretary, for one hundred per centum of the full financial obligations to be fulfilled by the contractor and for full observance of other obligations. The full terms of the performance security shall be determined by regulations.

[61] In 1991 a small group of insurgents launched an extraordinary brutal campaign of terror (including random shootings, rape, and chopping off hands) to gain control of these regions, recruiting child soldiers and enslaving

due to the weak transitions that have been overseen by the governments, with every new one seeking to create its own laws to regulate the energy industry in the country. Currently, the West African state ranks 176th out of 177 countries listed on the United Nations Development Index with the rule of law being one of the primary determinant factors for rating on the scale.

The same comparisons can be seen between Norway and Nigeria which are highly endowed with oil resources. On the one hand, Norway has transformed itself as one of the countries with the highest quality of life. On the other hand, Nigeria is notorious for its mismanagement of resource proceeds which have led to slow economic growth at best. It has a population of over 130 million people. In its early years of exploration between 1965 and 2000, the country experienced a decent percentage of its Gross Domestic Product from oil revenues. In spite of this wealth, the number of Nigerians categorized as living in extreme poverty increased by 34% from 19 million people to 90 million in the course of thirty years.

Nigeria has approximately 37.2 billion barrels[62] of proven oil reserves. The ownership and the control of all minerals, mineral oils and natural gas in the country have been vested in the Federal Government[63]. This is a close mirror of the situation in Kenya where the sector is owned by the Government on a trust basis for the people of Kenya. Further similarities with the legal framework in Nigeria and the current as well as the proposed legislation through the Energy Bill include:

1. The control by the Ministry of Petroleum which compares to the Energy ministry in Kenya in terms of mandate.

---

locals to work the diamond pits. With the money they received from selling these diamonds abroad, the insurgents bought enough weapons nearly to topple the government.
[62] This is the largest amount producer in the African continent and the 11th largest on the global scene
[63] Constitution of Nigeria, 1999

2. Nigerian National Petroleum Corporation (NNPC) which mirrors the National Oil Corporation of Kenya.

The Department of Petroleum Resources has been tasked with the primary goal of processing the applications for the licenses and the leases within the country's oil and gas industry.

Nigeria has consistently been labeled as a nation that is a victim of the resource curse. Worryingly, a critical examination indicates that the legislative framework has been duplicated in Kenya. To further heighten this anxious position, this paper estimates that the proposed Energy Bill will only serve to heighten expectations as was the case during the introduction of the Petroleum Industry in 2012. In both instances also, the relevant ministries have been tasked with the formulation as well as the implementation of the legislative policies that have been adopted in the sector.

Analytically, the only difference that seems to stand out from the legislative provisions of the two oil producing states is in environmental management. In Nigeria, the Environmental Impact Assessment Act of 1992 covers aspects of the environment and the impact of exploration on the environment. However, in Kenya, the environmental impact of oil and gas exploration seems to be generally provided for under the Petroleum Act, as well as under the proposed Energy Bill. The Environmental Management and Co-ordination Act of 1999 is gravely outdated and sparingly provides for the impact on upstream oil and gas exploration on the environment.

This paper contends that the huge discretionary power that has been afforded to the contracting parties[64] by both the current laws and the proposed Energy Bill offers potential conditions for the country spiraling into a resource curse nation. Further, the Kenyan system compares to a number of African state provisions that have been cited as being victims of the resource curse. Despite the progress that has been made by the African states in recognizing the rule of law, the legal frameworks still lack a definitive edge to warrant substantive growth within the energy sector. Part of this has been credited to the duplicating nature of the systems from other jurisdictions, mainly western, which fail to address the unique circumstances of the region.

Evidently, there is an operational uncertainty that stems from the extent of responsibility that has been mandated on either of the two levels of government. While the Draft National Policy recognizes this gap, it has not been formally adopted. The draft policy is also notable for pointing out that there lacks a legislative framework for the process of devolution in terms of the functions that have been assigned within the energy sector in a bid to ensure that there is a continuity of services within the sector as well as provide a guiding mechanism for the County governments for the devolved responsibility.

The various roles of the two levels of government within the energy sector have been provided for under the Fourth Schedule of the Constitution. This offers an operational uncertainty in terms of the extent of the respective responsibility to be allocated on each of the

---

[64] The Model Form Product Sharing Contract states that 'if after the effective date of this contract the economic benefits of a party are substantially affected by the promulgation of new laws and regulations, or of any amendments to the applicable laws and regulations of Kenya, the parties shall agree to make the necessary adjustments to the relevant provisions of this contract, observing the principle of mutual economic benefits of the parties.

level[65]. Further to this, it is worth noting that the Constitution places the authority of the management of minerals and mineral oils under the auspices of the National Land Commission[66].

This paper finds that this offers a breeding ground for potential conflict between the powers that have been conferred on the Cabinet Secretary in charge of Energy and Petroleum by virtue of the Petroleum Act alongside the powers that have been placed on the National Land Commission in relation to the administration of mineral oils. The next chapter of this paper analyzes the legal concerns of the local communities where the oil fields have been found, the legal provisions for their concerns and the legitimacy of their expectations.

---

[65] Despite the recognition of this gap by the National Energy Policy by pointing out that there is no framework for the devolution of functions within the energy sector in order to ensure that there is continuity of service, this framework is yet to be developed.
[66] Article 62(3), Constitution of Kenya 2010

4.0. CHAPTER FOUR

4.1 IMPACT BENEFIT AGREEMENTS IN ADDRESSING LOCAL COMMUNITY CONCERNS

To what extent can the legal framework legitimize the expectations of the local communities?

The Constitution of Kenya 2010, by providing for the enactment of laws to be adopted by parliament over specified periods of time, has compounded the already dire situation in Kenya over the supremacy of laws. With the steady interest in the upstream oil and gas sector, clear cut laws should be in existence outlining the legal scope of governance concerning the resources. Most of the laws have not yet been enacted. Further, the proposed legal frameworks are yet to be adopted. Additionally, the existing legislation provisions have not been aligned to the current constitution.

The expectation of the population cannot be over emphasized[67]. This is particularly so with regard to the improvement in the quality of life as a result of poverty alleviation due to the revenues derived from the oil and gas sector. A profound concern involves the communities living in the places where the discoveries have been made.

---

[67] Valentine Ataka, Impact Benefit Agreements as an answer to the Tullow-Turkana Woes available at http://www.academia.edu/oil&gas accessed 10April 2015

Humphrey's Journal on *Natural Resources, Conflict and Conflict Resolution* argues that in a majority of the cases, the resources are exploited in areas that are inhabited by marginalized communities. Although this position is not the general rule, it holds true for the Kenyan oil and gas sector. This position is exemplified by Akosua[68] in the sense that:

> "Although the discovery of oil creates a sense of hope and expectation that the revenue would lead to the development of local communities and countries as a whole, in most cases, this dream has remained illusory as the exploration of the oil resources has led to the destruction of local communities and anarchy in oil-producing developing countries[69]"

As noted by Valentine[70], the standoff between the Turkana community and Tullow Oil Plc offers a glimpse of what is expected if the legislative inadequacies on the exploration of oil and gas in the country are not addressed as a matter of urgency before production commences in 2019 as projected. The stand-off followed a mass protest owing to what the local community expressed as a failure by the company to employ enough locals. The region that is in dispute holds the largest basin in the discovery so far.[71]

The operations of Tullow Oil Plc within Kenya are governed by a Product Sharing Contract. This PSC is signed between the company and the national government. The standard Product Sharing Contract in Kenya provides that any company dealing with exploration and production of oil and gas resources has an obligation to employ Kenyan citizens in the petroleum

---

[68] Akosua Darkwah, *the impact of oil and gas discovery and exploration on communities with emphasis on women* available at http://www.g-rap.org/docs/oil_and_gas/netright-akosua_darkwah-2010.pdf accessed 13 April 2015
[69] Akosua Darkwah, *the impact of oil and gas discovery and exploration on communities with emphasis on women* available at http://www.g-rap.org/docs/oil_and_gas/netright-akosua_darkwah-2010.pdf accessed 13 April 2015
[70] Valentine Ataka, Impact Benefit Agreements as an answer to the Tullow-Turkana Woes available at http://www.academia.edu/oil&gas accessed 10April 2015
[71] Tullow Oil, 2013

operations, and until the expiry or termination of the contract, train those citizens[72]. This paper contends that this clause establishes the problem of local expectations versus legal reality which is the focus of this chapter.

First, the clause does not specify the proportions of the employment that is to be directed to the Kenyan citizens. Secondly, the generalization of the term "Kenyan citizen" as opposed to "local community" brings an aspect of the extent, and legitimacy of the expectations of the local community. While there is no basis for justification in any positive law for the local community members to be given first preference in employment matters, this is definitely a legitimate expectation. Without social acceptance, then the smooth operations of the exploration and production will be put to jeopardy.

It is notable that Tullow Oil Plc has committed itself to the International Voluntary Principles on Security and Human Rights[73]. While this essentially binds the company in addressing the basic problems plaguing the local Turkana community, the extent of such obligation has not been specified in any document. This has been left to the discretion of the company.

The current legal framework has not placed any provision for providing the local community with a platform in which they can negotiate measure or quantify the impact benefit of the operations of the oil and gas exploration process. Successful upstream sector in other countries and notably Angola have adopted the use of Impact Benefit Agreements. These address indigenous issues as an acceptable means of resource benefit sharing.

---

[72] Clause 13 of Kenya's standard Product Sharing Contract

[73] These are voluntary principles adopted by companies in the extractive and energy sectors on Security and Human Rights in pursuing an approach that addresses the root cause of the problems of the local community as opposed to applying a strict legal obligation.

This paper argues for the adoption of an IBA as a means of covering the legislative gap in addressing the expectations of the community. An IBA refers to a quasi-legal document that has been reached as a result of consultation concerning the proposed resource extraction, project or development that has the potential of impacting on the rights or interests of the local communities. IBA's have been credited with securing social acceptance of the upstream project as well as ensuring that the companies make legally binding commitments to meet the Community Social Responsibility obligations[74].

In addressing the legislative gap that has ominously been left in the legal drafts of the upstream sector, the agreements would include provisions on the free, prior and informed consent of the indigenous communities in relation to the activities that affect their lives. Further, this should provide for partnerships in the creation of local job opportunities and the development of all required skills within a specified time duration and any undertakings to develop the infrastructure that correspond with the local community needs. In addition to the above, this should also cater for the responsibilities of either party with regard to environmental protection, rehabilitation programs, and the exit strategy. Of equal importance, this would be the best avenue to provide for articulate provisions for the amicable and procedural dispute settling methods before resorting to the court process.

The crisis in Nigeria between the Ogoni[75] people has been directly linked to be as a result of the exploring companies' inadequacy in providing for the expectations of the community. BP Shell, the exploring company in this case was only interested in securing profits at the expense of

---

[74] The British Columbia aboriginal communities have adopted IBA's in oil and gas producing areas.
[75] Bloomfield, Steve (2008) 'The Niger Delta: The Curse of Black Gold'. The Independent.
http://www.independent.co.uk/news/world/africa/the-niger-delta-the-curse-of-the-black-gold-882384.html.
Accessed on 11 April 2015

the local community. In the compensation awarded by the Courts in the consequent case filed, it was held that the exploring company, although not bound by law, had an obligation to ensure that the concerns of the community are respected and upheld.

By extension, within the African context, the Ugandan border with the Democratic Republic of Congo where 3.5 billion barrels of oil have been discovered is also in dispute. The secession of South Sudan from Sudan where the latter now holds 75% of the total oil that that previously belonged to the former is also being disputed.[76] These examples highlight the seemingly unidentified problem over the ownership of oil resources.

This chapter concludes that the apparent lack of recognition of the local community interests in the upstream sector in any legislative document is another failure that needs to be addressed at the earliest opportunity. This paper prescribes the adoption of Impact Benefit Agreements in this regard.

---

[76] UK Energy Research Centre, 2009 available at http://www.opec.org/UKenergy.web/en/press_room/896.htm

5.0. CHAPTER FIVE

5.1. CONCLUSION AND RECOMMENDATIONS

5.1.1. Conclusion

Despite being at its nascent stage, this paper concludes that the current and proposed legal framework to manage the upstream oil and sector in Kenya, in the current form, is inadequate to comprehensively guide the country past the resource curse. In the current legal framework shape, Kenya would be better off without a further step in the murky world that is oil and gas production.

The exploitation of oil resources in Kenya has already started. The population, both locally and regionally have immense expectations owing to this development. Importantly, it is imperative that there is an assurance on the local communities on what precisely is to be expected in terms of the benefits and responsibilities to be expected. Critically, the loopholes that have been identified within the legal framework must be first acknowledged and addressed in order to avoid the resource curse.

While lauding the efforts that have thus far been achieved, a lot still needs to be done. This is especially in the enactment of laws governing the oil and gas sector, and by extension the energy sector to align with provisions of the Constitution. The Energy Bill has to be adopted at the earliest opportunity with a keen review on some of the contentious provisions. The National Energy Policy should equally be adopted with the efforts of all arms of government concerted to ensure the effective enforcement of the obligations that each of the arms has. Further, both the local and central government should work closely in order to ensure that the process of devolution attains its set objectives, which principally involve benefiting the citizenry.

5.1.2. Recommendations

Owing to the critical evaluation of the present model and comparison with the selected case studies, this paper makes the following recommendations for the upstream oil and gas energy sector in Kenya:

1. There is urgent need to improve the technology that is applied not only in the upstream sector, but also the downstream and middle stream sectors. Oil experts contend that with the adoption of proper technology, the oil and gas sector is made safer, the extraction process becomes cheaper and the quality of life of the general population increases. Some of the proposed technological improvements that Kenya could do with include:

   a. The Digital Oil Field[77]. This refers to a visualization platform that is web based and which can be used by companies in the management, measurement and tracking of the data from the oil and gas sector.

---

[77] Booz & Co, Unleashing Productivity: The Digital Oil Field Advantage. Available at: http://www.booz.com/media/uploads/UnleashingProductivity.pdf. [Accessed 23 April 2015].

b. The adoption of Cleantech[78] which is geared towards the reduction of the harmful effects of hydrocarbons.

2. The adoption of minimum standards to be adopted by nationally as concerns the oil and gas sector. These standards will guide the laws that are made by the County governments on the devolved responsibilities within the oil and gas sector. This will ensure the alignment of the laws that have been made at all levels.

3. Codification of the legal framework that governs the upstream oil and gas sector. In the present regime, the sector is regulated by laws that are not only outdated, but also fragmented.

4. Adoption of the Draft National Energy Policy as the principal policy framework for the energy sector in Kenya. Further, a complimentary policy framework should be adopted in light of the dual-government system in Kenya.

5. A clear definition of the policies that govern the sharing of revenues in the oil and gas sector. This should maintain a balance with other resources in that county.

6. Improving the strategies for the governance of the oil and gas sector. This should be achieved principally through legislative reforms. The *Angolanization* Policy for instance in Angola seeks to ensure that the benefits derived from oil production in the country is beneficial to the people.

---

[78] *http://www.cerionenergy.com/articles/34*. [Accessed: 23 April 2015].

Bibliography

BOOKS

Branch, D. (2011) *Kenya: Between Hope and Despair, 1963-2011* New Haven and London:

Yale University Press.

40

Collier, P. and A. Hoeffler (2004) '*Greed and Grievance in Civil War*' *Oxford Economic Papers*, 56 (4), pp. 563–595, DOI: 10.1093/oep/gpf064.

Collier, Paul. (2007). *The Bottom Billion: Why the Poorest Countries are failing and what can be done about it*. Oxford: Oxford University Press.

Collier, Paul and Anke Hoeffler (2000). *Greed and Grievance in Civil War*. Policy Research Working Paper 2355. Washington DC: World Bank

Frynas, Jedrezej, E. (2004). *The Oil Boom in Equatorial Guinea*. African Affairs 103 (413): 527-546.

Humphreys, M., W. A. Masters and M. E. Sandbu (2006) '*The Role of Leaders in Democratic Deliberations*. Results from a Field Experiment in Sao Tome and Principe', *World Politics*, 58, July, pp. 583-622, DOI:10.1353/wp.2007.0008.

Karl T. L(1997) *The Paradox of Plenty. Oil Booms and Petro States*. Berkeley-Los Angeles-London: University of California Press.

Watts M. (2009) 'Oil, development, and the politics of the bottom billion', *Macalester International*, 24, Article 11, pp. 79-13

Yav, Joseph. (2007) '*The Curse of Oil in the Great Lakes of Africa*'

REPORTS

Heya, M. (May 10, 2012) *Petroleum Exploration Overview in Kenya*, Presentation at the 19th Engineers International Conference. Ministry of Energy,

Kenya,http://www.powershow.com/view/3b0097NzgxM/19TH_ENGINEERS_INTERNATION AL_CONFERENCE_powerpoint_ppt_presentation

Nyoike, P. M. (2012) *Outlook of Oil and Gas Exploration Status in Kenya*, East Africa Upstream Summit, Nairobi, 25-26 October.

Tullow Oil (2013) *East Africa exploration and appraisal update,* Press Release, 21 February, http://www.tullowoil.com/index.asp?pageid=137&newsid=833 (accessed 22 October 2014)

United Nations Environmental Programme (2009) 'From Conflict to Peacebuilding; The Role of Natural Resources and Environment' UNEP.

United States Non-Governmental Delegation Report (1999) 'Oil for Nothing: Multinational Corporations, Environmental Destruction, Death and Impunity in the Niger Delta'

LEGISLATIONS

Constitution of Kenya (2010)

Income Tax Act Chapter 470 of the Laws of Kenya

Petroleum (Exploration and Production) Act, Chapter 308 of the Laws of Kenya.

Petroleum Development Fund Act, Chapter 426C of the Laws of Kenya.

The Draft National Energy Policy, 2012

JOURNALS

Anderson, D.M. and A. J. Browne (2011) '*The politics of oil in eastern Africa*', Journal of East Africa Studies, 5:2, pp. 369-410, DOI:10.1080/17531055.2011.573187.

   DOI : 10.1080/17531055.2011.573187

Arellano-Yanguas, J. (2011) '*Aggravating the Resource Curse: Decentralization, Mining and Conflict in Peru*', Journal of Development Studies, 47(4), pp. 617-638, DOI: 10.1080/00220381003706478.

Energy Literature 9 (1): 3-42.

Oil and Gas Journal, Vol 98, Issue 11.

OPEC, 2013 World Oil Outlook.

Palley, Thomas I. (2003) 'Lifting the Natural Resource Curse' Foreign Service Journal, 80

Petzet, A. (2011) 'Kenya: Remote Mandera basin block awarded', *Oil and Gas Journal*, 3 August,http://www.ogj.com/articles/2011/08/kenya-remote-mandera-basin-block- awarded.html (accessed 29 September 2014)

Stevens, Paul. (2003). Resource Impact: Curse or Blessing? A Literature Survey. Journal of the resource curse

INTERNATIONAL INSTRUMENTS

Energy Charter Treaty

WEBSITES

Commission of Revenue Allocation (2011) *Commission of Revenue Allocation. Promoting an*
 Equitable Society, http://www.crakenya.org/information/revenue-allocation-formula/
 (accessed 12 October 2014)

http://www.cerionenergy.com/articles/34. (Accessed: 7 April 2015)

http://www.globalpolicy.org/security/natres/oil/2007/1003greatlakes.htm. (Accessed on 17 April
2015)

http://www.iea.org/media/files/WEO2013_factsheets.pdf. (Accessed: 4 April,2015)

Oil and Gas Journal, Vol 98, Issue 11. http://www.ogj.com/oil-exploration-and
development/discoveries.html. (Accessed: 7 April, 2015)

www.globalpolicy.org (Accessed 24 April 2015)

DICTIONARIES

Black's Law Dictionary, 2nd Edition

Duhaime's Law Dictionary

Nolo's Dictionary of Law

NEWSPAPERS

NG'Asike, L. (2013) 'Turkana pastoralists oppose Tullow Oil proposal', *The Standard*, 29 July
 http://www.standardmedia.co.ke/business/article/2000089602/pastoralists-oppose-tullow-
 oil-proposal (accessed 29 September 2014)

Shikwati, James, Key Challenges Kenya is Likely to Face from Oil, Gas Discoveries, Standard

Newspaper,Friday,August2,2013.http://www.tullowoil.com/index.asp?pageid=137&category=ye

ar=Latest&month=&tags=84&newsid=675. [Accessed: 24 November 2013].